TREE TOPS

TREE TOPS

BY
JIM CORBETT

WITH AN INTRODUCTION BY
LORD HAILEY

Illustrated by Raymond Sheppard

GEOFFREY CUMBERLEGE
OXFORD UNIVERSITY PRESS
LONDON   NEW YORK   TORONTO
1955

Oxford University Press, Amen House, London, E.C.4
GLASGOW NEW YORK TORONTO MELBOURNE WELLINGTON
BOMBAY CALCUTTA MADRAS KARACHI CAPE TOWN IBADAN
Geoffrey Cumberlege, Publisher to the University

PRINTED IN GREAT BRITAIN

INTRODUCTION

JIM CORBETT's story of the visit paid by Her Majesty the Queen to Tree Tops in 1952 was written only a short time before his sudden death in Kenya on 19 April 1955. He was then nearing his eightieth year. When he had visited England in 1951 he had shown few signs of his age, but he had in fact never fully recovered from the effects of the severe illness from which he had suffered in Central India, in the course of training British troops in jungle fighting before they took part in the Burma Campaign.

I do not know how far the picture formed of him by his readers differs from that which will live in the memory of his friends. In one respect perhaps the reader who has known him through his books may have some advantage over them. He seldom spoke of the hardships and dangers of those encounters with man-eaters which gave such an incomparable thrill to his record of them. He felt, I think, that these were matters which lay between him and the great beasts whose strength and courage he respected, and whose lapses into ways that were a menace to man he could in due season forget.

Many of his acquaintances probably failed to realize that the name and deeds of this quiet and unassuming man were a household word among the hillfolk of the scattered hamlets of Kumaon. I doubt indeed if he would ever have given to the world the earliest of his books, *Man-eaters of Kumaon*, in 1944, had he not hoped that its publication might contribute something to the funds of St. Dunstan's, which had in the previous year opened a training school for blinded Indian soldiers. I remember how modest was his own estimate of what this contribution might be. He did not realize how enthralling were the stories he had to tell, nor how greatly their interest would be enhanced by his manner of telling them. Yet, as the world was soon to acknowledge, he possessed, in fact, that supreme art of narrative which owes nothing to conscious artistry.

Since, however, he is necessarily the centre of his own stories, they have much to reveal of his own history and way of life. Those who have read *My India* and *Jungle Lore* will not need to be told that he was one of a large family and was brought up during the summer months at the Himalayan hill station of Naini Tal, and in the winter on the small property held by his family at Kaladhungi in the foothills below it. Sport was in his blood, and from boyhood he set himself to gain that intimacy with the jungle and its life that he would need if he was to enjoy such sport as his modest means allowed. He never forgot in after life the habit which he then taught himself of noiseless movement in the jungle nor his rare understanding of its sights and sounds, and it was then that he began to acquire that unique combination of speed and accuracy in the use of the rifle to which he was later to owe so much. One who knew him at that period has said, however, that even in his youth he took no special pride in this achievement. Good shooting was to him an obligation rather than an accomplishment. If things were to be killed, then this should be done instantly, and without pain to them.

As soon as he left school at Naini Tal, he found employment with the Railway Department, at first in small posts but afterwards in charge of the transport at Mokameh Ghat, where the Ganges River created a broad gap between the two railway systems. There is a great bridge over the river now, but at that time more than half a million tons of traffic were ferried across it every year, and had to be transhipped from one gauge of rails to another. The conditions of work were exceptionally arduous, and that he carried it on for over twenty years was due not only to his power of physical endurance, but to his friendly personal contacts with the large force of Indian labour which he employed as contractor. They gave an unmistakable proof of their own feelings for him during the First World War. He helped to raise a Kumaon Labour Corps for service overseas, and took his section of it to France. It was then that his Indian subordinates at Mokameh Ghat arranged with the labourers that they would together carry on the work on his behalf throughout his absence. In the War he was given the substantive rank of Major in the Indian Army.

The nature of the work during these years gave him little leisure for sport, but during his holidays in Kumaon he was able on three occasions to answer the calls which were made on him for his help against man-eaters. Between the years 1907 and 1911 he disposed of the Champawat and Muktesar man-eaters and the Panar leopard. The first and last of these marauders were believed to have killed between them no fewer than 836 human beings, and they were perhaps the worst of the man-eaters from which Kumaon suffered in our generation, though others of a later date became more notorious. The leopard of Rudraprayag, for instance, which was officially recorded to have killed 150 human beings, acquired so wide a reputation in India because it preyed on the pilgrims who followed the route to a well-known Hindu shrine.

With his retirement from his work at Moka-meh Ghat there began a new chapter in his life. He was now his own master. His requirements were simple; he was unmarried, but he had at Naini Tal and Kaladhungi the devoted com-panionship of two sisters, one of whom (the Maggie to whom he so often refers) has sur-vived him. It was now that there occurred the majority of the encounters with man-eaters of which he has written in his books. The passing of the years did nothing to diminish the energy or the courage which he devoted to this task. The disposal of the Rudraprayag leopard, with its long tale of hard living and of sleepless nights, when Corbett was almost as often the hunted as the hunter, took place when he was fifty-one. The killing of the Thak tiger occurred when he was sixty-three. There seemed to be no limit to his endurance of fatigue or his ability to meet unruffled what seemed to be misfortune or mishap.

But there was another aspect also in the life which he now led. It seemed that sport, in the sense that the word is commonly used, had ceased to hold first place with him. So far as he was concerned, the tiger and the leopard at all events were immune, unless they were taking human life. Often when he and I were together, we were visited by deputations of the hillfolk asking for help; to be more correct, it was he that they sought out. He it was, as all their world knew, who had so often ventured his own life to save others in Kumaon from a Terror which filled their days and nights with fear. There was indeed here something that passed the ordinary bounds of human fear, for the ways of the ancient gods of the hills are unpredictable, and who could tell that the Terror was not a visitation from them? But the rubric that Corbett applied to the inquisition which was now opened was strict, however friendly and considerate in its terms. It was no use for them to plead their losses in cattle or goats. The tiger was lord of the jungle and must have its dues. Not until he himself was convinced that a tiger had been killing human beings, not by chance or in anger, but because it sought them as food, would he agree to come to their help.

One noticed, too, that the keen observation of jungle life that had once seemed to minister to sport now became of increasing interest for its own sake. There could be nothing more enjoyable than to spend in his company long days on the hillside or in the jungle, where every twisted twig, every call of bird or animal, seemed to carry its own meaning to him; or, if the interpretation was not at once clear, would provide him with matter for most engaging speculation. For him, this was not nature study, it was his world, and these were the things that meant life and death to its inhabitants. Photography became of greater concern than shooting. I recall an occasion when I chanced on him as he emerged in some apparent disorder from a tangled thicket in the jungle near Kaladhungi. He explained that he had been trying to get a picture of a tigress, but she was in a bad temper, and as often as he went into the thicket she drove him out again. He added, however, as one who was ready to make due allowances, that she had her cubs with her. This seemed to be typical of the terms on which he now stood with the animals of Kumaon. There was an understanding which would justify the tigress in demonstrating against the intrusion on her nursery. But the matter need not be carried further.

When during the Second World War he gave the Government his services in training troops in jungle fighting, he received the honorary rank of Lieutenant-Colonel, and in 1946 there was conferred on him the distinction of the Companionship of the Indian Empire. The Government had previously allowed him a privilege which he valued very highly when it gave him the 'freedom of the jungle', or, in other words, the liberty of entry to all its Forest Reserves. I do not need to speak here of the regard in which he came to be held by the people of Kumaon. As kindly and generous as he was fearless, he gave freely of himself, and asked nothing in return. But I think that in the olden days he would have been one of the small band of Europeans whose memory has been worshipped by Indians as that of men who were in some measure also gods.

When so many of his friends left India in 1947, he and his sister decided to leave also, and made their home at Nyeri in Kenya. It could not have been an easy decision for him to make. He loved his home in Kaladhungi as greatly as he was himself beloved by its villagers. But Kenya could at all events minister to his passion for photographing wild life, and he was able to indulge it to the full. The proximity of Tree Tops to Nyeri made him a frequent visitor there, and it is pleasant to know that we have now his own story of the visit of Her Majesty the Queen to Tree Tops, for the letters which he wrote at the time to his friends showed how very deeply moved he was by his experiences as a member of her party.

London   **HAILEY**
September 1955

TREE TOPS

A BRILLIANT sun was shining in a deep blue sky and the air was crisp and invigorating, on that fifth day of February 1952.

I was standing on a wooden platform, thirty feet above ground, and before me stretched an oval-shaped clearing in the forest, two hundred yards long and a hundred yards wide. A miniature lake with tall tufts of grass dotted on it occupied two-thirds of this open space, the rest consisted of a salt-lick. On the farther margin of the lake a snow-white heron stood motionless, waiting patiently for the approach of unwary frogs, and in the open water in front of it a pair of dabchicks were taking their young brood of four, which looked no bigger than marbles, on what was evidently their first excursion into a danger-filled world. On the salt-lick a solitary rhino was moving restlessly, occasionally stooping to lick the salt ground and then throwing his head to snuff the wind that was blowing down towards him from the forest.

The lake and the salt-lick were surrounded on three sides by dense tree forests and on the

B

fourth, and farthest from me, by a hundred-yard-wide strip of grass which came right down to the margin of the lake. Beyond the strip of grass, and forming a frame for it, was a belt of Cape Chestnuts. These chestnuts were in full bloom, and sporting among the blue tinged with purple flowers was a troop of colobus monkeys which, with their flowing white tails and long white mantles hanging from their shoulders, looked like giant butterflies as they flitted from tree to tree. A more beautiful and a more peaceful scene it would not have been possible to conceive; and yet not all was peace, for in the dense forest beyond the monkeys was a herd of elephants and in the herd was discord. Every few minutes the air was rent by loud trumpeting mingled with the screaming and deep rumbling of angry elephants. As the sounds of strife drew nearer, the monkeys collected in a group and after barking in alarm flitted away over the tree-tops, led by a mother who had a young babe clinging to her breast. The solitary rhino now decided his need of salt had been met and snorting his defiance he turned in one movement, as only a rhino can turn, and with head held high and tail in the air, trotted into the forest on the

left. Only the heron, still patient and unre-
warded, and the family of dabchicks, remained
unaffected by the approaching herd. Presently
out of the dense forest the elephants began to
appear, not in Indian file but on a broad front of
fifty yards. Silent now, and unhurried, in twos
and threes they drifted on to the bush-dotted
strip of grass, while my eyes ranged back and
forth until I had counted forty-seven. The last
to come into the open were three bulls, one
quite evidently the master of the herd and the
other two younger brothers, or possibly sons,
who were approaching the time when they
would wrest the mastery of the herd from their
elder, and drive him into exile.

At the far end of the platform on which I was
standing a short flight of steps led up into the
hut which is known to all the world as 'Tree
Tops'. The hut is built in
the upper branches of a
giant ficus tree and is
only accessible by a steep
and narrow thirty-foot-
long ladder. Time was
when, for the safety of
the occupants of the

hut, the foot of the ladder was cranked by a winch into the upper branches of an adjoining tree, but this safety device had long since been discontinued. The accommodation of the hut consisted of a dining-room, in one corner of which was recessed a wood-burning stove, three bedrooms for visitors, a narrow slip of a room for the White Hunter, and a long open balcony provided with comfortable cushioned seats. From the balcony there was a clear and uninterrupted view of the miniature lake, the salt-lick, and of the forest beyond, with the Aberdare mountains in the background rising to a height of 14,000 feet.

*　　*　　*

PRINCESS ELIZABETH and the Duke of Edinburgh had arrived at the Royal Lodge, Sagana, twenty miles from Nyeri, two days before, and on that February morning I had just finished shaving when I received a breath-taking telephone message informing me that Her Royal Highness had been graciously pleased to invite me to accompany her to Tree Tops. The Royal Party were to leave the Lodge at 1 p.m. and, driving slowly, arrive at 2 p.m. at Tree Tops where I was to meet them.

Nyeri has one of the finest polo grounds in Kenya and the previous day a match in which the Duke had taken part had been played there, with the Princess watching. The polo ground is eight miles from Nyeri and fifteen miles from the Royal Lodge, and is surrounded on three sides by forest and high grass. Neither my sister Maggie nor I feel happy in a crowd, so while the populace from far and wide was collecting at the polo ground for the great event, we motored to a bridge spanning a deep ravine which runs through dense forest towards the ground. Though a state of emergency had not up to that time been declared, security measures were being taken, for the unrest had started and there had been in the neighbourhood a number of cases of arson about which the press, for obvious reasons, had kept silent. I was uneasy about the deep ravine which afforded an easy approach to the polo ground. However, on examining the stretches of sand in it I was relieved to find no footprints, so we spent the rest of the evening near the bridge, keeping watch on the ravine. This accounts for our absence from the polo match.

* * *

AFTER receiving the telephone message I shaved a second time, had breakfast, and then went to the administrative headquarters to get a road pass, for I had to use the road that had been closed for the Royal Party. At midday I motored eight miles along the main road and, leaving it at the polo ground, took a rough track which runs for two miles up a narrow valley to the foot of the Tree Tops hill. Here, where the track ends and a narrow footpath winds up the hill through dense cover for six hundred yards to Tree Tops, I removed my handbag and British warm from the car, and sent it back to Nyeri. To a number of trees adjoining the path, slats of wood had been nailed to form ladders as a means of escape in the event of attack by elephants, rhino, or buffaloes. It is a sobering fact that two days after that path had been traversed by the Princess and her party, four of the biggest trees to which ladders were nailed were uprooted by elephants.

*   *   *

IT was now 1.30 p.m. on that fifth day of February, and 2 p.m. was zero hour. The elephants, still silent and peaceful, were quietly browsing on the grass and bushes while slowly drifting down towards the lake, and it was possible to observe them more closely. They were of all sizes and of all ages, and five of the cows were accompanied by calves only a few weeks old. These five cows, and the three bulls, who were in that seasonal condition known as 'must', were a potential danger. However, if the herd remained on the far side of the lake for another thirty minutes, all would be well. The minutes dragged by, as they do in times of strain, and when only fifteen remained the elephants started to edge down towards the salt-lick. This salt-lick extended to within a few yards of the ficus tree, and from the projecting balcony it was possible to drop a handkerchief on to any animal on the lick below. Between the lick and the tree a few small branches had been laid, to form a screen for people approaching the ladder leading to the hut above. These branches had been crushed down by elephants and other animals and, at the time I am writing of, the screen was a screen only in name.

On the platform, with the passing of every moment, my anxiety was growing. The herd of forty-seven elephants was crowded together on the salt-lick. It was zero hour and the Royal Party, if it was up to time, would now be on the path, and at that moment the big bull elephant, annoyed by the attention the two young bulls were paying to one of the cows, charged them and all three enraged animals dashed into the forest on the left, trumpeting and screaming with rage, and started to circle round at the back of Tree Tops, *and in the direction of the path.* Would the escort with the Royal Party, on hearing the elephants, decide that it was too dangerous

to go forward and so return to the comparative safety of the open ground where they had alighted from their cars, or would they take the risk of trying to reach the ladder leading up to the hut? Crossing the platform, I peered into the forest. From the foot of the ladder the path ran for forty yards in a straight line, and then curved out of sight to the left. Terrifying sounds were to be heard in plenty but nothing was to be seen on the path, and there was nothing that could be done. Presently I caught sight of a man carrying a rifle at the ready, followed closely by a small trim figure. The party had arrived, and on reaching the bend in the path, from where the elephants on the salt-lick were in full view, came to a halt. No time was to be lost, so, slipping down the ladder, I approached the small figure which, from her photographs, I recognized as Princess Elizabeth. Smiling her greeting, and without a moment's hesitation, the Princess walked unhurriedly straight towards the elephants which were now crowded at the hut end of the salt-lick, and within ten yards of the foot of the ladder. Handing her handbag and camera to me, the Princess climbed the steep ladder, followed by

Lady Pamela Mountbatten, the Duke, and Commander Parker. The escort, led by Edward Windley, then turned and retraced their steps down the footpath.

In the course of a long lifetime I have seen some courageous acts, but few to compare with what I witnessed on that fifth day of February. The Princess and her companions, who had never previously been on foot in an African forest, had set out that glorious day to go peacefully to Tree Tops and, from the moment they left, their ears had been assailed—as they told me later—by the rampaging of angry elephants. In single file, and through dense bush where visibility in places was limited to a yard or two, they went towards those sounds, which grew more awe-inspiring the nearer they approached them. And then, when they came to the bend in the path and within sight of the elephants, they found that they would have to approach within ten yards of them to reach the safety of the ladder. A minute after climbing the ladder the Princess was sitting on the balcony and, with steady hands, was filming the elephants.

It was not usual for elephants to be seen at Tree Tops at that time of the day and, while they were being filmed, they did all that elephants could be expected to do. The old bull returned to the herd, followed at a respectful distance by the two young bulls, and he again chased them away, to the accompaniment of loud trumpeting and angry screaming. A flock of doves alighted on an open patch of ground, and on seeing them one of the elephants filled its trunk with dust and, cautiously approaching, discharged the dust at them, for all the world like a man discharging a gun loaded with black powder. The doves were doing no harm and it was out of sheer mischief that the elephant frightened them away, for after doing so it flicked its trunk up and down as if laughing and flapped its ears with delight. The Duke witnessed this side-play with great amusement and when the doves returned and the same elephant, or it may have been another, again sucked dust into its trunk and approached the birds he drew the Princess's attention to the scene, which she filmed. A cow elephant now came towards us with the smallest of the calves close to her side. Stopping a few yards in front of the balcony the

mother pressed the damp tip of her trunk on to
the salt-impregnated dust, and then conveyed it
to her mouth. The calf, taking advantage of
its mother's preoccupation, inserted its head
under her left foreleg and started to suckle.
Greatly interested in this filial scene the Prin-
cess, who had her eye to her cine-camera, ex-
claimed, 'Oh, look. It is going to drive the baby
away!' This was said as a small elephant,
three or four years of age, trotted up to the
mother and inserting its head under her right
foreleg, also started to feed. The mother stood
perfectly still while the meal was in progress
and when the baby and its elder sister had had
enough, or possibly when there was no more to
be had, the mother disengaged herself and
passing under the balcony, accompanied by the
baby, went out on to a spit of land jutting into
the lake. Here she had a drink, sucking the
water into her trunk, raising her head, and
pouring it down her throat. After quenching
her thirst she walked into the lake for a few
yards and then stood still. Left to itself the
baby got nervous and started to squeal in a thin
small voice. To the cry for help the mother
paid not the least attention, for this was a

lesson that it was safe for the young to follow where the mother led. Eventually the baby summoned sufficient courage to wade into the water, and when it was within reach the mother tenderly drew it to her and, supporting it with her trunk, gently propelled it to the far bank.

When watching a herd of elephants it is intensely interesting to see how kind they are to the young. Bored with standing about while their elders are feeding, the young play about and get in the way. When this happens, even with great terrifying-looking bulls, the young are gently put aside, and are never struck or trodden on. Of all the animals in the wild, elephants have the most real family or herd life. When a female retires for maternity reasons the elders of her own sex are always on hand to keep her company and to protect the young, and until the new arrival is able to walk the herd remains in the vicinity. If young or old get into difficulties or are threatened with danger, real or imaginary, the others rally round to give what help they can. It is for this reason that herds in which there are young are avoided, and it was for

the same reason that the approach to the ladder was dangerous, for if the wind had changed, or if a nervous cow with a very young calf had seen the party, there would have been grave risk of an attack. Fortunately the wind did not change and by approaching the elephants unhurriedly and noiselessly the Princess and her companions avoided detection.

Karra, a big male baboon who had recently lost a part of his upper lip in a fight, which gave him a very sinister look, now led his family of eleven down a forest track to the edge of the salt-lick. Here they halted, for elephants dislike baboons and I have seen them chase such a family into trees and then shake the trees in an attempt to dislodge them. Karra was taking no risks on this occasion. After surveying the scene he led his family back into the forest and, circling round the salt-lick, approached the ficus tree from the left. A bold young female now left the family and, climbing one of the wooden supports of the hut, arrived on the balcony. Running along the railing, and avoiding dislodging the cameras and field-glasses placed on it, she gained a branch of the ficus tree jutting out from the hut. Here she was rewarded with a sweet potato nearly as big as her head and while she sat contentedly peeling it with her teeth was filmed and photographed at a range of a few feet.

*   *   *

TIME slipped by unnoticed, and when the Princess was told that tea was ready in the dining-room, she said, 'Oh, please may I have it here? I don't want to miss one moment of this.' While tea was being taken, the elephants drifted off the salt-lick, some going into the forest on the left, and others passing under the balcony and going along the shore of the lake to the right. The Princess had laid her tea-cup aside and was looking at a sheaf of photographs, when I saw two male waterbuck racing at full speed down a forest glade towards the salt-lick. On my drawing the Princess's attention to the two animals, she reached for her camera, and the photographs slipped from her lap to the floor. Saying a word or two, amply justified in the circumstances, the Princess got her camera to her eye just as the two bucks, with only a length between them, dashed with a great splash into the lake. When the leading one had covered

about forty yards it stumbled over a sunken tree-stump, and without a moment's hesitation the one behind plunged its horns into it. One horn entered the unfortunate animal's left buttock, while the other went between its legs and into its stomach. So firmly fixed were the horns that their owner was dragged forward for a short distance before it could free itself. The wounded animal plunged on until it reached the shelter of a big tuft of grass. Here where the water was up to its neck it halted, while the aggressor circled round through shallow water and after shaking its head in defiance walked off into the forest. This incident, which was evidently the final act in a battle that had started in the forest, had been filmed by the Princess and now, laying her camera aside, she picked up her field-glasses. Presently passing the glasses to me, she asked, 'Is that blood? Do you think it will die?' Yes, it was blood. The water all round was red with it and, judging by the laboured way in which the stricken animal was breathing, I said I thought it would die.

Karra and his family, who had been joined at the salt-lick by five warthogs and a dainty young doe bushbuck, were now causing a diversion.

c

Two teenage females were competing for the affections of a boy friend, whom both of them claimed, and this was causing angry scenes and a lot of screaming. Karra would have settled the dispute by chastising all three of the young ones if he had not at the time been contentedly lying in the sun—being filmed—while one of his wives ran her fingers through his thick fur, looking for the things that were irritating his skin and which it was her wifely duty to find and remove. While this was going on, the five warthogs were down on their knees cropping the short grass on the edge of the salt-lick, and the youngest of Karra's children was industriously trying to climb up the young doe's hind-legs in order to catch its tail. Every time an attempt was made the doe skipped aside, enjoying the game as much as the onlookers.

Neither the Princess nor the Duke smokes, so, as I am addicted to this pernicious habit, I left my seat near the Princess and went to the end of the balcony, where I was presently joined by the Duke. In the course of our conversation I told him that I knew Eric Shipton, that I had read the articles in *The Times* relating to the Abominable Snowman, and that

I had seen the photographs taken by Shipton of the footprints in the snow. Asked if I had any theories about the Abominable Snowman, I told the Duke, much to his amusement, that I did not believe that the tracks in the snow photographed by Shipton had been made by a four-legged creature, and that while I would not dream of accusing Shipton of a leg-pull, I had a suspicion that his own leg had been pulled. I went on to say that knowing the great interest that was being taken in the snowman I was disappointed that Shipton had not followed the tracks back to see where they had come from, and forward to see where they led to. This, the Duke said, was a question he himself had put to Shipton, and that Shipton had told him the tracks had come from the direction of wind-swept rocks which had no snow on them, and that they led to other rocks devoid of snow where it was not possible to follow them.

*   *   *

WITH the passage of time, the shadows were beginning to lengthen. More animals, more in fact than had ever before been seen at Tree Tops, were

coming out of the forest on to the open ground. In the slanting rays of the sun these animals, together with the massed bloom of the Cape Chestnuts, reflected in the still waters of the lake, presented a picture of peace and of beauty which only an inspired artist could have painted, and to which no words of mine could do justice.

On rejoining the Princess she again handed me her field-glasses, and said, 'I think the poor thing is dead.' The stricken waterbuck did indeed look dead, but presently it raised its head from the tuft of grass on which it was resting and, struggling to the bank, lay with its neck stretched out and its chin resting on the ground. After it had been lying without movement in this position for a few minutes, three elephants went up and, stretching out their trunks, smelt it from head to tail. Not liking what they smelt they shook their heads in disapproval and quietly walked away. From the fact that the buck had not reacted in any way to the presence of the elephants we concluded that it was now dead, so Commander Parker and I went to look at it. While we were going through the hut and climbing down the ladder, the dead animal was

dragged away—possibly by the two leopards whose pug marks I had seen on the path when going to Tree Tops—for all we found on reaching the spot was a pool of blood. Close to the pool of blood was a big bush behind which the partly eaten remains of the waterbuck were found next day.

Throughout the afternoon and evening the Princess made detailed notes of all the events she had witnessed, and of all the animals she filmed. These notes I knew were intended as a running commentary for those at home who would see her films while she was on her visit to Australia—the visit that did not take place.

As the beautiful sunset faded out of the sky and the soft light of the moon illuminated the scene, cameras were put away and we talked in hushed voices suiting our surroundings and the subjects we talked on. I told the Princess how grieved I had been to hear of her father's illness, and how greatly I rejoiced that he was again well enough to indulge in his favourite sport, bird-shooting. And I told her how distressed I had been to learn from the B.B.C.'s broadcast that her father had stood hatless in a bitter cold wind to wave to her as she left the

London airport. On my expressing the hope that he had not caught cold, she said that he was like that; he never thought of himself. The Princess then told me of her father's long illness, their anxieties, their fears, their hopes, and their joy when one day he put his walking-stick to his shoulder and said, 'I believe I could shoot now.' This was hailed as a turning-point in his illness, and a token that he had taken a new grip on life. The Princess asked me if I had ever shot grouse, and when I told her I had tried to do so, with little success, she said that I would know how difficult they are to shoot and would therefore have some idea of how well the King shot when she told me that on the first day he went out he shot, from one butt alone, forty-three birds. That was more, I told her, than I had shot in a week from many butts. The Princess rejoined that her father was a very good shot. She then told me where her father had been shooting on that fifth day of February, and where he intended shooting on the following day.

I have heard it said, and have seen it stated, that when the Princess waved goodbye to His Majesty the King at the London airport on her departure for Australia, she knew she would never see him again on earth. This I do not believe. I am convinced that the young Princess who spoke of her father that night with such great affection and pride, and who expressed the fervent hope that she would find him quite recovered on her return, never had the least suspicion that she would not see him again.

*   *   *

DINNER was now announced and, leaving the balcony, we filed into the dining-room. Covers had been laid for the seven people present, and as I moved to the farther end of the room, the Princess said, 'Won't you come and sit between us?' As she said this, the Duke indicated the cushioned seat that had been prepared for him and took the uncushioned seat next to it. On either side of the long unpolished dining-table were benches made, I am sure, of the hardest wood the Duke has ever sat on. Eric and Lady Bettie Walker were our hosts and the sumptuous repast they provided was greatly appreciated, for the excitements of the day and the fresh clean air of the forest had given everyone a keen appetite. While coffee was being made on the table, the spirit lamp caught fire, and was swept off the table on to the grass-matted floor. As frantic efforts were being made to stamp out the blaze the African boy who had served dinner unhurriedly came forward, extinguished the flames with a wet cloth, retired to his cubbyhole behind the stove, and a minute later replaced the lamp refilled and re-lit on the table. Not long after, Tree Tops was raided and that very efficient boy was carried off, together with all the bedding, provisions, cooking utensils, and other movable articles in the hut, and it is left to conjecture whether the boy's bones are bleaching in the African sun, or whether he became a terrorist.

After dinner the Princess and her party returned to the balcony. In the dim light of the moon nine rhino could be seen on the salt-lick. The heron and the family of dabchicks, the elephants, and the other animals, had all retired and the frogs that had been so vocal earlier were now silent.

Leaving the Royal Party on the balcony, where they stayed until the moon set, and taking my old British warm which had served me well during the war years, I went down and made myself comfortable on the top step of the thirty-foot ladder. I had spent so many long nights on the branches of trees that a few hours on the step of a ladder was no hardship; in fact it was on this occasion a pleasure. A pleasure to feel that I would have the honour of guarding for one night the life of a very gracious lady who, in God's good time, would sit on the throne of England. And after that day of days I needed to be left in quietness with my thoughts.

The moon set and in the heart of the forest the night was intensely dark. Visibility was nil but that did not matter, for with the exception of a snake nothing could climb the ladder without my feeling the vibration. Within a few inches of my face, and visible against the sky through a break in the foliage of the ficus tree, was hanging a manila rope which went over a pulley and was used for hauling up baggage and provisions from the ground to the rooms above. Presently, and without my having heard a sound, this rope was agitated. Something moving on soft feet had laid a hand on it, or had brushed against it. A few tense moments passed, but there was no vibration on the ladder, and then the rope was agitated again for the second time. Possibly one of the leopards whose pug marks I had seen on the path had come to the ladder and on finding it occupied had gone away. The ladder, though steep, would have offered 'no obstacle to an animal with the climbing ability of a leopard, and for all I knew to the contrary the platform above me may have been used by leopards as an observation post, or as a place on which to sleep at night. In contrast with an Indian jungle the African forest is disappointingly silent at night and, except for an occasional quarrel among the rhinos, all I heard throughout the night was the mournful call of a hyena, the bark of a bushbuck, and the cry of a tree hyrax.

At the first glimmer of dawn I washed and shaved, and on going up to the hut found the Princess sitting on the balcony with a meter in her hand, testing the light before making a film record of an old rhino that was on the salt-lick. Daylight comes rapidly in Africa, and when the first rays of the sun lit up the scene before her, the Princess started to take the picture she had been waiting for. While she was filming the rhino the Duke drew her attention to a second rhino that was coming down to the salt-lick. The two animals were evidently old enemies, for they ran at each other in a very aggressive manner and for a time it appeared that a great fight would be staged for the benefit of the Royal onlookers. Advancing and retreating like experienced boxers manoeuvring for position, the two rhinos sparred round each other until the newcomer decided that discretion was preferable to valour and, with a final snort of defiance, trotted back into the forest, giving the Princess an opportunity of drinking the welcome hot tea that Lady Bettie was handing round.

Though she had spent so few hours in sleep the Princess had started that second day with eyes sparkling and a face as fresh as a flower. No artificial aids were needed or used to enhance the bloom on her cheeks. Many years previously I had stood one winter's day on the banks of the Ganges with the Princess's grandfather, and looking at her now it was easy to see from whom she had inherited her beautiful colouring.

With the rhinos gone and only the white heron standing

motionless on the margin of the lake and the family of dabchicks cutting furrows across its smooth surface, cameras and field-glasses were put away and we went to the dining-room for breakfast, which consisted of scrambled eggs and bacon, toast, marmalade, and coffee made this time without mishap, and the choicest and most luscious fruit that Africa could provide. There was no need now to talk in hushed voices, and as we finished breakfast I remarked that the Princess was the only member of her family who had ever slept in a tree, or eaten a dinner and a breakfast prepared in one.

The escort that was to conduct the Royal Party through the forest to the waiting cars now arrived, led by Edward Windley, and as the radiantly happy Princess drove away she waved her hand and called out, 'I will come again.' Soon after her return to the Royal Lodge the Princess was told that her father, of whom she had spoken with such affection and pride, had died in his sleep during the previous night.

I do not think that any two young people have ever spent such happy and carefree hours as Princess Elizabeth and Duke Philip spent at Tree Tops, from 2 p.m. on 5 February to 10 a.m. on 6 February. For myself, those hours that I was honoured and privileged to spend in their company will remain with me while memory lasts.

A register is kept of visitors to Tree Tops, and of the animals seen. The day after the Princess visited Tree Tops the register was brought to me to write up. After recording the names of the Royal Party, the animals seen, and the incidents connected with them, I wrote:

> For the first time in the history of the world a young girl climbed into a tree one day a Princess, and after having what she described as her most thrilling experience she climbed down from the tree the next day a Queen—God bless her.

* * *

ALL that now remains of the ficus tree and the hut honoured by Princess Elizabeth and the Duke of Edinburgh, and visited for a quarter of a century by thousands of people from all parts of the world, is a dead and blackened stump standing in a bed of ashes. From those ashes a new Tree Tops will one day arise, and from

another balcony a new generation will view other birds and animals. But for those of us who knew the grand old tree and the friendly hut, Tree Tops has gone for ever.

NYERI

6 *April* 1955

PRINTED IN
GREAT BRITAIN
BY
WESTERN
PRINTING SERVICES
BRISTOL